THE RESCUE
OF LUMINOUS BEING

TONY VACCA

This book is dedicated to those who fall so completely in love with our precious and unfinished humanity that they will not back off nor back down when it is time to speak up and act on behalf of the freedoms that freedom brings. It is dedicated to those who won't "wait in the car when you tell them to wait in the car," (RIP Sekou Sundiata) and most especially to those who see the light of our luminous being as the force that guides them so far beyond where we are right now, and so very clearly towards where we are so very ready to arrive.

It is dedicated to those who acted as my encouraging spirit-angels, whose thoughtful comments and insightful brainstorms reminded me that we are here to do all we can to live up to how we want to be. Sometimes they did that just by being who and how they are; from life companions to treasured collaborators. Sometimes they playfully jumped on the moving bus of my visions and rode a few miles just to light up the ride. But most times we were all swimming in the intoxicating waters of the collective effects we have on each other and pretty much anyone nearby... and I am so very grateful for every one of them, and for all of this. They all know who they are, and if you know me, you know who they are too. If you're wondering if you are among this group... you probably are, and by the time you read these words, I will have told you.

Special thanks to the entire poetic team for our group creation of "You and Me and All Humanity" and "Things Gotta Change." I am so blessed to work with them and to have their contributions included here. They are: Tantra Zawadi, Mamadou Ndiaye, Bideew Bou Bess, and Abiodun Oyewole.

Published by Human Error Publishing

www.humanerrorpublishing.com
paul@humanerrorpublishing.com

Copyright © 2022
by
Human Error Publishing & Tony Vacca

All Rights Reserved

ISBN#: 978-1-948521-71-0

All photos and images by Tony Vacca.

Graphic assistance and double-cool helpful guidance
by Larry Chernicoff at: windhorsecreative.com

Human Error Publishing asks that no part of this publication be reproduced or transmitted in any form or by any means electronic or mechanical, including photocopy, recording or information storage or retrieval system without permission in writing from Tony Vacca and Human Error Publishing. The reasons for this are to help support the publisher and the artists.

THE RESCUE OF LUMINOUS BEING

TONY VACCA

TABLE OF CONTENTS

My Soul Likes to Travel 2
If I Could Make It Rain 4
You and Me and All Humanity 6
You Don't Know Me 10
BLUE, BLUE, AND MORE BLUE 14
Blank Slate 16
21st Century Recalculations 18
Things Gotta Change 20
everything changes everything 24
Standing In The Rain 27
We Human Beings 28
River 30
I Am A Child of The 60's 32
The Origin of Rain 35
Questions Concerning The Weight of Things 36
My Dreams Take Me Over 38
Wonder and Miracle 40
Night Spirits 42
Undertow of Survival 43
Legacy of Freedom 46
I Just Go Missing 48
The Great Rejoining 49
Air Pilgrimage 52
Planet of Miracles 54
It's Going To Happen 56

This is a **book of words.**

My words.

Magical tangles of ink on paper for the benefit **of** our fluid souls.

i o**ff**e**r** this and all I hav**e e**ver create**d** as evidence **o**f our **m** a g n i f i c e n t h u m a n i t y, and of what I see as the **world wide attempted rescue** of

o u r

t r u l y l u m i n o u s b e i n g.

MY SOUL LIKES TO TRAVEL

I am tangled up in the webwork of the universe, in the ebb and flow of my breath. I am swimming in the whispers of visions that caress my sorrows while I sleep under the blanket of the heavens. There are prayers in the roaring ocean waves, there are unasked questions in the moonlight... there are stars whose ancient energy promises the rescue of our luminous being. I am a collision of forces that have found their way to awareness... to mystery... to light.

And all this... all of this is the spiritual thunderstorm, the whirl of dark translucent clouds, the luscious waterfall of human voices carrying me towards what I know of love, what I feel of gratitude, and towards miracle and wonderment. I feel pushed to the edge... but ready to fly. I feel like a gathering of forces and elements whose nature is this loose and momentary confluence that I call my body... and my mind.

But my soul... my soul likes to travel in the exquisite nothingness of long before. Before me, before you, before this and all this is. Before beginning and ending... before being and becoming. My soul likes to travel the endless nothingness of forever... and ever... and ever...

My soul likes to travel the earth and sky to places near and far and so totally beyond my reach. My soul likes to travel the depths of love to the timeless embrace of you and I. My soul likes to travel eye to eye to the mystery of being and being so alive. My soul likes to travel the early morning light and be bathed in the sweet wonderment of another day.

My soul likes to travel the webwork of our miracle humanity and the tangle of our inter-connected languages. My soul likes to travel with the first kiss of soon-to-be lovers, hanging on every word, on every need to be touched and known, and on every chance to lift our spirits to the heavens and dance, and sing and re-jump for joy.

Oh Yeah...my soul likes to travel.

My soul likes to travel the infinity of night in an ocean of stars surrounded by worlds beyond any easy comprehension. My soul likes to travel the terrain of my fingertips whose touch conveys whole new worlds of wonder. My soul likes to travel the whispy clouds that are the breath of this earth and the respiration of this living planet, just like, just like my soul likes to travel among the angels as they accompany our arrivals and departures, our loves and our losses, our laughter and our every moment under the influence of awe.

My soul likes to travel at the edge of sunrise, where the sky begins to whisper the first rumors of light and where the pure blue-black of night lets go of its hold on darkness. My soul likes to travel up through the shallow waters near the shore and burst into the first light of summer. My soul likes to travel along the flight paths of music imagined and made real by those so totally under the influence of our eternal rhythms.

My soul likes to travel the long forgotten waterways of deserts that were once great forests. My soul likes to travel in the footsteps of dinosaurs and ancestors, of soothsayers and prayer-makers, of story-keepers and rule-breakers… My soul likes to travel far beyond the wings of flying creatures and into the heaven for dreams.

My soul likes to travel on empty pockets, on the wet and luscious overflow of darkness and rain in a forgotten forest. My soul likes to travel lost and found and totally under the influence of gratitude.

My soul's travels have taken me to injured and forgotten, into the labyrinth of fear and abandonment, into the jagged terrain of love badly lost and no way home… and still my soul likes to travel in the rivers of our tears and in the rivers of prayers we send to the heavens, to ourselves, and to each other, asking to be forever guided towards the light, forever in each other's thoughts and embraces, and forever and ever riding the ride of our traveling souls.

My soul likes to travel…. across time and space, through dark and light, deep into the nothingness of eternity and back again to the on-and-on of on-and-on… through spirit and emptiness, through the weave and sparkle of consciousness as I seek and I am sought, as I teach and I am taught, as I love and I am loved by the nature of our nature, by the pathos our being, and by how and why my soul… likes to travel.

I've seen us breathe new life into our bodies by the magnetism of our souls… I've felt the heartbreak of our attempted self-denial and the self-defeating pretense of ineptitude. I've watched us avoid our reflections for fear of catching a glimpse of our magnificent humanity… and I've seen myself and us all rise up from impossible just to behold the awe and the roar of creation that surrounds us, and that we now have to fully claim to be within us.

It's time to ride in the jet-stream of our being… It's time to kiss and make love to our dreams… It's time for us to embrace the sorrow and the joy of leaving behind all that has brought us here… so we can re-claim and freely travel our unknowable future.

It's time…it's time…it's time.

IF I COULD MAKE IT RAIN

There is something about rain that just sets my spirit free. The feel of rain on my upturned face, as if each drop was a kiss of liquid sky to help me balance on my way through a precarious world.

I hear there are places on this water-planet where rain is so very rare, where water is a miraculous and transformative elixir… where beings look to the skies with hope… with worry and with wonderment… and I watch myself gather in a delicate whisper of a thought, something like "what if we could bring the rain?"

I can't help thinking there are those who say "we have done such things."

My mind swirls into a fast-forward through the space/time continuum and I'm staring into sun-lit clouds, under the influence of flying high in the skies above America… I'm looking down onto lands so very blessed… and then fast forward and I'm home and thrown into a world overflowing with the machinery of mass distraction, where dreams slip through the graceful hands of so many who've never really been immersed in the deep waters of our luminous being.

In this place… in this place I call home, rain is the plaything of children whose delirious laughter is all part of their ritual celebration. They are dancing in the liquid gold matrix of the most precious life-giving commodity in all the cosmos… dancing as if all they knew was the deep oneness of all things… while so many of their elders sleep-walk in a spiritual free-fall in a land where… where everything is possible.

The genii of my child-mind conjures me one wish right out of thin wet air and I hear myself say… If I could make it rain… If I could make it rain in this place…the rain would fall across this water-blue planet and we would wash the blood off bloodstained city streets where the horrors of war have sometimes twisted love to hate, have threatened to crush our precious embrace of the next generation and fill their hopeful eyes with the blood shot terror of destruction.

If I could make it rain the clouds would cry until the machinery and minions of war fall to rust and ruin, until the new-green of a thousand plants re-weaves our precious web of life, until flowers reclaim the concrete, making a new terrain so sweet that all creatures who gather there are filled with wonder and dreams of how new things might grow from within them, of how new realities always transform from the old, and how even death will bow… and worship… and embrace the perpetual lunge of all things towards life.

If I could make it rain, the feathery cargo of our souls would gently float downstream on a caravan of forest leaves, back to the oceans of our beginnings, back to the glimmer and sparkle of the first living things, back to the time before mind and so forward into the re-minding, as in re-minding us all in the now of now, that we are among the great miracles of a wondrous cosmos.

I would want the rain to find us finding our way together, filling the air with our music, filling our souls with songs of wonder, filling our minds with bold visions of past and future worlds, healing our wounds and growing lush gardens where love flourishes and fills the next generation with dreams… only they can realize.

If I could make it rain… I'd make it rain like this… and we would be forever more immersed in miracle, where our forever minds would wander endlessly into the wet inviting oneness of rain.

…and we would drink in these waters.

Every rain drop would carry the sun's glow from above the dark gathering clouds, covering the earth with it's sparkling energy, and filling the souls of each living being with an energy beyond comprehension to be perpetually shared and re-shared among us all in an eternal rebirth of wonder.

Yeah baby. Let it Rain. So … yeah. Let It Rain… Let it Rain…

YOU AND ME AND ALL HUMANITY

THE GROUP COLLABORATIVE VERSION:

(This is a collaborative poem featuring Mamadou Ndiaye, Tantra Zawadi, Tony Vacca, Bideew Bou Bess, and Abiodun Oyewole.)

(Mamadou Ndiaye)
Salam (peace)

(Tantra Zawadi)
Time to stand up for all humanity… You and me.

(Mamadou Ndiaye)
I'm the missing piece of the World Peace, CEASE FIRE! You're the missing piece. I don't want to live this fantasy life, turn up your light, stand for your rights.

(Tony Vacca)
Whether you stand up tall or take a knee,
Ain't no wrong way to honor our humanity.
We are miracle creatures, look at us and you'll see
something magic about love and how we
can go soul to soul, and eye-to-eye,
looking for wisdom till the day we die.
From "peace and love" to "on and on," from "gonna take you higher,"
to "above and beyond the beyond."

(Tantra Zawadi)
Miracle talk of a spiritual kind, escaping the prisons of a colonized mind.

(Tony Vacca)
Turn up the volume on our sweet energy, it's all about how we set ourselves free. We're in this together, you and me, time to stand up and live up to how we want to be…

CHORUS
You and me and all humanity,
time to stand up and live up to how we want to be.

You and me and all humanity,
time to live up to how we want to be.
You and me and all humanity,
time to stand up and live up to how we want to be.
You and me and all humanity…

(Tantra Zawadi)
Time to live up to how we want to be. Miracle talk of a spiritual kind, escaping the prisons of a colonized mind. Cosmic wonders of souls lost, blinded, hoodwinked, smacked, shackled, and tricked into darkness. What's going on planet earth? Children of spirit?
Time to make a move and embrace the questions.

At the beginning and the end, LOVE is the lesson. Kissing the universe with unparalleled intimacy that reaches beyond our future dreams.

You and Me and All Humanity, time to stand up and live up to how we want to be. You and Me and All Humanity, time to live up to how we want to be.

Our real history founded on truth and positivity. From the lips of griots pledging allegiance to the common good. Spiritual creatures disrupting institutions and misguided political perspectives… transforming this gift of life with the magical consciousness of love.

Time to live up to how we want to be. Descendants of all that is magnificent, third-eye-free. It's time for you and me, representatives of all humanity to live up, to show up, and kiss all humanity. You and Me and All Humanity, time to stand up and live up to how we want to be.

CHORUS
You and Me and All Humanity,
time to stand up and live up to how we want to be.
You and me and all humanity,
time to live up to how we want to be.
You and Me and All Humanity,
time to stand up and live up to how we want to be.
You and me and all humanity, time to live up to how we want to be.

(Tony Vacca)
Time to kiss the earth, live up to your dreams.
Everything is even more than everything seems.
Sun and moon, the earth and sky,
it's a paradise planet once you and I realize
nothing is beyond our infinite reach.
We are the spirit creatures we hope to be.
We are the children of earth, descendants of stars
We know what war is, we bear the scars
but the light of love is what I see,
time to live up to how we want to be…
You and me and all humanity, time to live up to how we want to be.

(Bideew Bou Bess) *translated from Wolof*
Stand up, and speak up, sing out in harmony. Stand up, and speak up, sing out in harmony. Together we help us all to be strong, to find our way, we all belong to our human family, every woman and man can see together we are the future of humanity…

(Mamadou Ndiaye)
I'm the missing piece of the World Peace, CEASE FIRE! You're the missing piece. I don't want to live this fantasy life, turn up your light, stand for your rights. Get up humanity, show your positivity, Rise up humanity, show your unity. We're going nowhere if you're lost in negativity. Jammala nexh. Peace is so beautiful.

You and Me and All Humanity, time to stand up and live up to how we want to be. You and me and all humanity, time to live up to how we want to be.

(Abiodun Oyewole)
So let it be that we cherish the humanity we see in everyone who breathes. Life should not be to deceive… be a blessing to each other, treat each other like a sister or brother. Be the light we were meant to be. Love and nurture our humanity.

We are here to make our dreams come true and do all the good things we want to do. Let this human connection give us direction to a higher place where we can heal, and feel the love for the entire human race.

You and Me and All Humanity,
time to stand up and live up to how we want to be.
You and me and all humanity, time to live up to how we want to be.

You and Me and All Humanity,
time to stand up and live up to how we want to be.
You and me and all humanity, time to live up to how we want to be.

YOU DON'T KNOW ME

Spring of 2000, in the Philly train station, complete with a 20 foot high bronze angel holding a fallen soul in her strong arms. Her wings are open and ready. There's a distraught equanimity to her gaze, and she seems to be looking at everyone… everyone in this very large station. She is a luminous presence.

I am in this station, waiting for someone to arrive… someone I have totally fallen in love with… and I feel so very connected and so very alone.

I look across the many faces in this wide open, mostly empty room where so little happens and so much is anticipated, and I imagine the telepathic calls we are sending out to ourselves and to others… so much like this guardian unseen-angel of souls calling out to each of us… and mostly going unheard.

I try to listen in for what she might be saying, but she's not using words. What I am hearing though, what I am hearing are delicate undefended monologues rising like prayers to the heavens, rising like beacons of light in a storm, from traveling souls in search of a place to go…

I hear them, like… like "I see you looking. You don't know me. I walk through the halls of our giant train stations, I sleep on the wooden benches, worn beautiful and smooth by the countless others who've passed here before me; by generations who were probably waiting for the sight and sound of someone they love. But me, I'm just here holding on to whatever I can. You don't know me."

And then another…

"You don't know me… I sit alone with my headphones cranking the music of the streets that I know, calling to me to survive another day. I'm tuned in, but running out of time. I'm thinking maybe those who sat here before me hummed the songs of their lives just under their breaths to accompany them in these moments of such strange lonliness… So yeah, maybe I'm wishing I was waiting for someone I love, like maybe they were wishing they were waiting for someone they love… and it hits me that you and others are looking at me like you know me or something… but hey, HEY, you don't know me."

And another…

"You don't know me… I have just enough energy to get on the bus to get to the train station. Just enough energy left in my arms, my legs and in my heart to make one more journey home to where they all know me. To where we talk about and remember times long gone just like they were yesterday. To where the loves lost and found resonate loud and true. To where some tears will find their way from the sadness I've known… find their way down my wrinkled face and somehow heal the pains of what I've lost by being part of so much that I've gained by being so very alive… I laugh more than you think, I cry more than I want to admit, I've seen more, risked more, lost more and found more than anyone even knows.

But right now… right now I sit alone on this hard bench that's even older than I am. I hear the sounds of lives so much younger than mine, I feel the energy of the people, the roar of the trains, and the purr of my sweet memories that are mine and mine alone to share when the moment comes. I look around at the people here when they're not looking. I suppose they look at me.

A lot of people in this world.

And then I realize, then I realize that so many of you… so many of you… you don't know me.

You don't know me."

BLUE, BLUE, AND MORE BLUE #2

Blue, blue, and more blue, into the infinite chaos of Divinity, into the infinite divine chaos of all things… blue, blue, and more blue into the infinite Waters of our beginnings, into the embrace of oblivion, as in before we come to life in this place of wonder and miracle, of suffering and ecstasy.

Deep, deep blue, blue, and more blue, like drowning in the welcome-blue of my lover's eyes, like swimming in the healing waters of earth, like the blue-black of space, space and more space, into the heavens, blue, blue and more blue, like the blue of the Blues, like the deep blue of a mother's whisper of love, like the blue of deep waters, and the Deep waters of surrendering to the blue oblivion of surrender.

Blue, blue, and more blue, like the waters of an angry sea, or like the healing waters of a dream. Blue like the iridescent soul-blue of one soul on ice, like the cold steel of a warrior's blade, like the deep blue of a bruised and broken heart.

Blue like the endless sky, like the infinite, deep waters of sorrow for the loss of love, or the loss of those we love. Blue like the cool waters of my mind, like the blue of the night sky reflected in one tear as it hits the floor. Blue, blue and more, more blue, blue, and more blue…

Until
the last star
in a sea of stars
disappears
into
the cool,
deep-blue
kiss
of infinity.

BLANK SLATE

I am a blank slate of wonder… a 548 mile-per-hour passenger on flight 2418. I am in a twilight zone of cloud and color, and under the spell of Alice Coltrane's music of ecstacy. I am under the illusion that I am floating, and in way over my head over an ocean of vapor and wonderment.

The horizon is divided into all things above and below the clouds. It's earth and sky, it's blinding white under endless blue, blue, and more blue, into the infinite sacred chaos of all things.

I'm at thirty-three thousand feet, hurtling through the luscious atmosphere above what I call my home… and I can't see our petty complaints. I can't see our significant others. I can't see our wondrous creations nor the horror of our wars.

I can't see our car loans and compound interest, I can't see the axis of evil nor the Tao te Ching. I can't hear the anguish of our lost loves, nor the cries of ecstasy from the healing touch of passion. I can't see the scams and schemes, I can't feel the crush of dreams denied. I can't hear the drums, nor the voices of the faithful singing their prayers. I can't see the children's eyes. I can't feel the hopes and pride of young parents. I can't see the barred windows on our inner city schools, I can't see the drug deals and cheap highs that insult our strengths and our ability to survive through the living hell of misfortune beyond our cruelest fears.

I can't see the self-inflicted wounds of self-denial. I can't see the triumph of getting back up after we fall. I can't see where my life unraveled, nor where I found the strength to find my way. I can't see the life-long friendships held together by love and selfless honor. I can't feel the swing of Ellington and Basie. I can't hear the groove laid down by Bernard Purdie behind Aretha Franklin. I can't see the soul of Marvin Gaye. I can't even feel the silk-lined glide of the Temptations.

I can't see Rahsaan Roland Kirk, (Mr. Blind Seer behind those dark glasses) coming back from a stroke and still kicking ass with his music. I can't even see where Don Cherry is buried, and all the beautiful, multi-kulti magic of his musical being.

I can't see the arrogance and petty thievery. I can't hear the lies and collusion, I can't see the genocide, the drug and oil wars, the killing fields… I can't see the way-back spin on a Pedro Martinez curve-ball. I can't hear the fiery words of The Last Poets. I can't see the barbed-wire of hatred. I can't feel the raw silk of sex with those we love. I can't hear the sweet devotion in our calls to prayer. I can't hear our conversations and confessions to ourselves, spun under the influence and in the illusion that we are speaking to God…

But from up here… even from way up here… I can almost sense our immeasurable strengths, and our undeniable optimism that we have literally written into the stone work of our creations. From up here I can just begin to see the curve of the earth, and the wondrous chaos of our journey through space on this one-and-only planet that is our home.

I can see the evidence of forces from which we are made and to which we return, and I can ride, I can ride this steel-winged bird of my flight home like I ride the rocket of my instincts, the rocket of my mind, and the rocket of my soul… into what there is of heaven.

21ST CENTURY RE-CALCULATIONS....

It would seem that I am a bystander in the hyper-cyber of the 21st Century... and it's trying so hard to fill my mind and empty my soul of its otherwise intrinsically valuable contents. I've heard we've got Wi-Fi at my Body/Mind Repair Shop, but I'm still struggling to get a clear enough signal to fully enable my extra-sensory perceptions in an honest effort to polish my soul.

I've posted and shared my life and I've even partially funded my visions on a cyber-cloud... that seems to mostly rain and thunder on the parade of my otherwise semi-magical reality.

Now, don't get me wrong... I see and truly enjoy the sweet smiles of the new-next hyper-tech generation. They are kinda cool in their own way. All of a sudden I hear the seductive voice of my inner-spirit guide; she is ticker-taping a message for me and it says... it says, "I dig where all this just might take us... but if our ever-evolving technologies fail to support our ever-evolving humanity, then I want no part of this Brave New World detour."

You know... you know sometimes I think I can see and hear the faint whisper of the word "dinosaur" as it scrolls just behind the eyes of, well pretty much anyone under 20... as if "dinosaur" is their best easy-access description of who and what I seem to be to them. Hey, maybe they're right. Maybe I am a lost traveler... you know, a fully committed soul on a disoriented express in search of the temple of our limitless humanity.

So I turn down the noise of all this 21st century machinery-in-motion; I turn down the deafening, obscene buzz of our appliances and the lifeless ice-blue glow of our ubiquitous devices... and I hear the distant call of... gongs... gongs, man. I sense and then I see the first light of a new day. I feel the sweet, sinewy, luscious sex of our interconnected minds and bodies in a web of connection... It's calling me... calling me, and I am fully immersed in the liquid being of our wondrous souls.

Yeah, I mean I have travelled in the Mother Lands of Human Beginnings… I have danced and felt the embrace of our perpetual oneness… and I have fallen, I have fallen completely in love with how exquisitely irresistible we are to one another.

The feel of a smile crosses what's left of my self's consciousness. And then, from way, way, way beneath the ruble and debris of the 21 Century… I hear the pseudo-soothing, Euro-hip nondescript female voice of my discarded GPS… She's saying, "Recalculating… recalculating… recalc…" But I'm still swimming in the deep and delicious sound of g o n g s)))))))))))))))). Gongs, man.

Dinosaur. Dinosaur? Me? Really? How about Multi-Culti Astral Traveler? Y e a h….   Recalculate that.

THINGS GOTTA CHANGE

This is a collective, poetic call created by Bideew Bou Bess (Moctar Sall, Baidy Sall and Ibrahima Sall), Tantra Zawadi, Tony Vacca, Mamadou Ndiaye, and Abiodun Oyewole.

(Bideew Bou Bess)
Ah yay yela yay… hey, things gotta change. Ah yay yela yay… Oh, things gotta change. Ah yay yela yay… hey, things gotta change. Everywhere we go, things gotta change. Yeah, here we are sending out greetings to one and all. We're right here on the mic saying how are you doing today? Listen up, we can all see, it's always time to make change that takes us further on the road to peace. Time to make clearer your mind, make clearer your soul. All this and more is right here for us all, you and me and everyone… it's a time for change.

(Tantra Zawadi)
Young minds, fertile and anxious to deliver truths passed down from griots with open minds, prophesying on street-corners, in townships and villages, about movements and phrases, finding ways to celebrate the rhythm of humanity… and change.

Shattering glass with our third eye for a clearer view of real love… How many dreams must die for poems of life to rise?

Things… things… Things gotta change.

Although we struggle to survive, we thrive in clay, steel, and concrete, through the valleys, deserts and homelands… love provides, and is sufficient to grow soulful beings, capable of letting go and letting live… Purpose being freedom, we believe. For every man and woman, every land and nation can join hands and lift their voices for a cause, because some things, some things… Some things gotta change.

How many dreams must die for poems of life to rise? For the fight is purely spiritual. Our souls are at stake and baby, baby, baby… Some things gotta change… Some… things… gotta…change. Some… things…gotta… change.

(Tony Vacca)
Hearts and minds gathered here to find the sound,
to put the rhythms and the words down,
to rock the time and open your mind,
to re-align our visions and set our minds on peace.

World hanging by a thread-bare thread,
some nearly gone, some already dead,
I'm not looking for trouble, it's already found me,
I'm not trying to bust your bubble but I can see
things gotta change… In every village and city in the world
there's gonna be love.

(Mamadou Ndiaye)
We want to talk about something. We're fighting every day for change. The word on the street is the world in my rap, and it's the message we're here to pass on. Listen: Everything's gotta change today. Every human being has a chance today. Look at yourself in the mirror. You're the one who can change tomorrow. The best of me is not something I take off when I shower. That's the way it is. Dig deep in your heart. Let's stop all this self-defeating madness.There's craziness going on, the world's a mess. If we're going to get to where we want to be, peace is what will lead us there.

(Tony Vacca)
In every village and city in the world there's always going to be love…
I see there are troubles to face and rise above,
ain't no trouble can erase the power of love
to free our minds and open our hearts
to start today to make a new start,
to find a way to heal the past,
to love every moment and make love last,
to honor the lessons of loss and pain
and hear me when I tell you again and again. We are the change…

Suma harit Abiodun… Abiodun Oyewole of The Last Poets taking us way back, to the way they did it in the way, way back…

(Abiodun Oyewole)
Revolution… There will be a revolution… and we will take it to the streets, armed with the knowledge and the love we have, spitting flames of truth, melting away the frozen dreams that never had a chance to come true.

There will be a revolution… governments will collapse like a deck of cards and the King and Queen won't exist anymore. Class will be something everyone has. Wealth will be judged by your deeds that turn a frown into a smile, a weed into a flower, and hope into reality.

There will be a revolution… what once was small will be big, what once was silent will be heard. Whoever is hungry will be fed. Diseases won't sell as commercials, and pain won't be our closest friend, and all the scars on our bodies and minds will heal, and will become the mirror of a beauty not seen or felt before… shining in our eyes, blossoming in our smile.

There will be a revolution… and children will be wise again. Our ancestors always speak through them, and we must listen. Fairy tales will not exist. The magic of us will make the impossible possible, the unreachable reachable, and turn the nightmare into a dream with an unshakable faith walking by our side.
There will be a revolution… oh yes, blood will be shed, lives will be lost, bullets will fly, bombs will drop, buildings will be set on fire, laws will be broken, lives will be shattered, deceit will be left standing in the rain. Major battles will be fought… inside of us… inside of us… and we will regain the trust of ourselves and each other.

There will be a revolution… And we… will… win.

We will win… we will win… we will win… we will win… we will win… we will win…

everything changes everything

Blood red line on the horizon,
I'm five miles high and riding
this steel-winged fuselage at the edge
of earth and sky, of wonder and fear as I
scan the clouds above this place I call home.
I feel its embrace, but I'm traveling alone
through this life and this delicate envelope of air.

The sky lights up a miracle blue,
the silk-orange streaks of light pass through
the remains of another night.
And I dream I am in your playful embrace,
the feel of your skin, the look on your face
and I'm home, though I'm hurtling through space
under and over the clouds of this truly wondrous place.

The sun is glaring in on me,
I'm staring back at infinity
through the luminous glow of love.
And I'm loving what has come to me
through grace and chance, and yeah I can see
an army of angels of mercy
hovering around our souls…

We're cursed, we're blessed, we lose our way,
we're put to the test and survive each day.
We're designed to live beyond all we know
of horrors and misery and then go
deeper into all it means just to be alive.

We pray, we drum, we chant, we sing,
we die and come back, and everything
changes everything…

We seek and find, we search and destroy,
we love and lose, we are the joyful noise
of humanity, left staring into the mystery

of the horizon, of dream, of consciousness,
of rise and fall and the chaotic mess
of this sweet paradise planet.
The sex, the drugs, the rock and roll,
the funky effect of digging your soul
in a galaxy of possible realities,
and the inevitability of opposing possibilities.
The up and down, the in and out,
the endlessness of "what's this all about?"
The hip, the square, the endless fall,
just being there and digging it all,
feeling high, like on the day you were born.

The earth and sky, the sun and moon,
the what and why, the how and who,
the second, the moment, the minute, the hour,
the destructive tendency to analyze and devour.
The presence of love, like the source of the Nile
is one precious raindrop, one delicate smile…

and here I am

five miles high and among the clouds,
I'm alone and wondering why this shroud
of sadness hovers over me
and our miracle planet, and yeah I can see
we're all woven into one sweet tapestry
of wonder and flaw, and our collective divinity,
our holographic humanity is the living one-ness of God.

Each day, each night washes over me,
It's fight or flight into infinity,
it's life and death and whatever's next,
it's peace and the unimaginable endlessness
of unimaginable endlessness, as the sun becomes
a blood red line on the horizon.
I'm five miles high and I'm riding

the question of how and why I still feel your embrace
the touch of your skin, the look on your face.
I am high and among the clouds in this truly wondrous place.

The sky lights up a miracle-blue,
the silk-orange streaks of light pass through
all I know of love and loss, of touch and go,
of heart and mind, of ebb and flow,
as each day, each night washes over me.
It's fight or flight into infinity.
It's life and death and whatever's next,
it's peace, and the unimaginable endlessness of unimaginable
e n d l e s s n e s s . . . . . .

The sun is glaring in on me.
I'm staring back at infinity
through the luminous glow of love.
And I'm loving what has come to me
through chance and grace, and yeah I can see
an army of angels of mercy
hovering end l e s s l y around our souls.

STANDING IN THE RAIN

He was standing in the rain… eyes turned up to the sky. His arms were open wide, like an old-timey antenna, in search of a signal that just might gather enough invisible energy to form a coherent image. Every drop of rain was a teardrop of cosmic possibility, as he gazed to the skies and into the ever-deepening blue of infinity.

One by one these precious droplets found him. They were whispers that cooled his skin, blurring and finally annihilating any separation between him and the forever changing flow of an ever changing everything.

These sweet waters rolled down his face… He cried in empathy with a crying sky that formed
the mystic envelope of life on this living, breathing third-sphere-from-the-sun. These were the original tears of joy, from which all others flow into the rivers that carry us forward and deeper into the great reservoir of being… and then somehow back again into the ribbons of energy from which we began.

He felt the cascade of rhythms as each piece of the falling liquid sky kissed his skin, as he danced among the patterns of their patterns… as he savored their overlapping starbursts, like the caress of a fading moment… again… and again.

He was standing in the rain among a billion breathing creatures on a living breathing planet that was circling a tiny star at the edge of a remote galaxy, virtually lost in a sea of galaxies forming an ever-expanding cosmos that itself

was a tiny raindrop on the face of God.

WE HUMAN BEINGS

Seems like we human beings are just about the most unlikely of occurrences in the entire cosmos. We are adaptive, nomadic creatures and our ancestors populated the earth by their endless journeys. Today the fate of the peoples of this planet are more inter-connected than any time in our history. Our survival literally depends on if and how we use our great diversity, our considerable knowledge and our collective wisdom to share the treasures of our world and become... something even more than we are now.

The petty fighting between the good peoples of this paradise place is a sad, heart wrenching sub-plot in our magnificent story. So yeah, I am painfully aware of the treachery and deceit, the greed and the horror, the manipulations, the bamboozlry and the malicious self-destructive meglo-maniacal bullshit. I have seen all that. It makes headlines, it takes space, and it sucks up spirit-energy beyond the deepest of deep black Black Holes in a cosmos of miraculous transformations.

But it's a small and insignificant spec on our good deeds, our thoughtful prayers, our visible and invisible heroics, our unbreakable friendships, our big, bold, all-inclusive visions, our songs, our poems, our healing touch, our rights of passage, our ritual celebrations, and our love... our unfathomable love.

All this is the connective tissue of all living things... All this is the sea of entropic energy that lights up our souls and all things seen and unseen. All this is the matter of miracles from which we come and to which we return. All this is our inheritance, to be held with care like we cradle our children; to be whispered to under the influence of love as we whisper to our beloveds; to be committed to as when we take a leap of faith into the realm of unknown certainties with the full-hearted intoxicating confidence that impossible leaps... must
be taken.

We are so very ready to go so very far beyond where we have traveled so very long to arrive. The journey has been to be ready for journey.

So where are we now? Is that the question? Where are we now?

I say we are standing in the doorway of Humanity's wildest dreams… that we can live in the deep and lasting embrace of our connection to this miracle planet and to each other; that our collective wisdom can guide us towards realizing, protecting, and sharing the treasure of our abundant resources, and that our ever-evolving technologies can truly and completely serve our ever-evolving humanity.

We are so very close…

Maybe… maybe all that remains to be done to realize all this is to, well… commit to going for it; to conscientiously align our efforts towards reclaiming our enlightened state of being… to speak more of our visions and less of our fears… and to point the arrow of our intensions directly at the vision of a future we have already dreamed.

So… pull the plug on the world-wide conspiracy to gather all the bad news and stuff it down our throats… pull the plug on the disgraceful hesitation tango of self-defeating self-doubt, and let's get on with the exquisite work of claiming our true and magnificent nature…

Bring on miracle and wonder. All things actually are possible.

RIVER

I walk along the edge of a river that was once spectacular and graceful. It meandered through marshlands at sunrise… it called out for joy as its frozen fingers thawed and broke free in spring… it whispered the quiet sensuality of its summertime flow… it teemed with life's battles and mysteries, a self-contained world within itself; the culmination of unknowable millennia collapsing in on itself until this instant.

I walk and walk along the edge of a river, now scarred and abused by creatures who like to call themselves wise and intelligent, who see themselves as the stewards of this miracle planet, spinning its magic in a far corner of miracle space. I walk along the edge of a river that is still willing to speak to me, and I hear its stories of how it nurtured and supported the living entities that came to it for survival, and then found so much more.

I walk along the edge of a river that knows the earth as a lover knows the contours of his beloved. Its flow has guided countless inhabitants back to the sea of our beginnings, to the first home of all living things. And this river breathes hopeful embraces on all who would love its meandering nature. This river purrs its welcome to all who would share and respect its treasure. This river makes love to its lovers, offering sustenance and safety and wonders beyond easy comprehension. The stars have learned to dance the surface of its silk and flow on moonless nights, and melt into the patterns of the wind, blurring memory and time like a long, slow, luscious true-love kiss…

I walk along the edge of a river. I wade into its secrets. I have seen my tears of sorrow and joy ride its promise to return home to the sea. I have run my fingers through the liquid mystery of its waters, I have tasted the transparent and wondrous essence of this rarest of all cosmic elements, and I know… I know that my living, breathing consciousness has its source in the flow of this magnificence.

I AM A CHILD OF THE 60's.

I am a child of the 60's… I mean, look at me. I look like that, I act like that, I play my music like that… I am a child of the 60's. I grew up just outside of Newark, New Jersey… Yeah, THAT Newark. Race riots, crime central for the Sopranos, and oh yeah, home to New Jersey's very own version of The Bottom Billion.

So try to imagine… I'm 7 years old and my mother brings me to the movies in downtown Newark to see the latest from Walt Disney. I come out of the theater and I hit the streets all starry-eyed and Magic Kingdom and… PAAYA! PAAYA! PAAYA! Two men running full-speed down the street. The guy with the gun's like 10 feet behind the other and he's missing with every shot. Stray bullets flying everywhere, people running for their lives, and I'm heading… towards the mayhem.

"Hey mom look at this, these guys are…"

Next thing I know my mother's got me in a bear hug and yanks me around the corner to safety… "ANTHONY, WHAT ARE YOU DOING?" "Mom, I gotta see this. These guys are shooting at each other, I want to…" "THIS IS REAL, BABY. LOOK AT ME… LOOK. AT. ME. YOU COULD GET KILLED!!!" I've never seen that look in her eyes. She's afraid… Oh, she's afraid I'll get shot and die right there in her arms. The world… just looks…different.

Now fast forward to 1967. It's "The Summer of Love" as in Peace and Love, and flower children and music festivals everywhere… And Newark, NJ sets itself on fire… on fire from racism, from fear, from trouble deep in the hearts and minds of America, and on fire "with liberty and justice" … denied.

Flames are dancing across my face and I'm looking out my back window and across the river to Newark. I can smell the burn of self destruction, and it says that so much more than a city is going up in flames… Tears are rolling down my face, and now I'M afraid. I am afraid for what all this might mean to my multi-culti rat-pack of childhood friends. We are the sons and daughters of mostly first and second generation immigrants, fighting for our lives… And, whoa, whoa…

All of a sudden it hits me.

The African-American kids in our sweet little circle… their ancestors had been born in this land long, long before any of the rest of ours had arrived. Come to think of it, their ancestors were stolen into this, beaten into this, and while we are all playing our part in this emerging America, I'm pretty sure it was from the blood, sweat and tears of a whole lot of their ancestors that a whole lot of this nation got built.

But somehow… somehow we make this our neighborhood. We walk these streets together, we go to the same schools together, we're on the same sports teams together… After the big game we drink from the same one-and-only soda bottle we got.

But I'm ashamed to say that sometimes… sometimes we throw down and are smacked right back by the racial and ethnic slurs of the day: Guinea! WOP! Jap! Chink! Mic! Spic! Nigg//-and we pretend like, "you know, that don't mean nothing" … but that's a lie, that's a big lie. Every one of those words were born of hatred, and every one of those words cut deep… and still…still we share our little corner of a broken world… with the world of us, but…
But we do not share the real and horrific legacy of enslavement, we do not go to the same barbershops, we do not argue over which girls to ask out on a date 'cause… you know. Every one of us has been knocked TO OUR KNEES by the free-flow of low expectations, and yet we do not kneel down together and pray at the same churches.

One more fast forward… one year later, 1968… and the crown prince of peace in the America I thought we were living in… is shot dead. Martin Luther King is shot dead… and for me it brings up a whole litany of "shot dead" in America. Like JFK shot dead… like four little Black girls go to church in Alabama and get blown to what's left of heaven… Like Malcolm X shot dead, like Black Panthers shot dead, like Robert Kennedy shot dead… like four peace-nik students at Kent State University shot dead, like Detroit like Johannesburg, like Newark just like Johannesburg, like freedom ain't nothing but a word, ain't nothing but a

Word.
Shot.
Dead.

What about freedom? What about land of the free? Somebody, anybody tell me, what about the promises we've made to each other from "Sea to Shinning Sea?" WHAT ABOUT FREEDOM?

But… it's too late. I've already seen that we are miracle creatures on a miracle planet in a miracle universe. And I have fallen completely in love with our exquisite, unfinished humanity.

So I just close my eyes and call up the one and only prayer my generation all knows and can sing together… c'mon people… "Come on people now, smile on your brother, everybody get together, try and love one another…

right
now.

THE ORIGIN OF RAIN

Somewhere in a remote corner of infinite space, water fell from the sky on the upturned faces of miracle beings. Their once fertile lands had forgotten the kiss of rain and rivers had lost their magic and flow... Forests were shape-shifting into grasslands, and into arid open vistas and then into deserts.

But this... this was the rain he kept dreaming of... This was the reach of forces connecting earth to sky, as if these droplets were liquid meteors from deep space, purposed for the rescue of luminous being among the creatures and peoples of earth.

This was water returning to dry lands. This was a transformative moment where the look, the feel, the smell and the possibility of all things... became real. This was the re-imagining of a flourishing earth, and all of this was in every drop that caressed his face. He played and re-played the super slo-mo cascade of these tear-drop promises as they danced their free-fall through the timeless air, and onto his cheeks, his forehead, and his lips. He cupped his hands and bathed his mind in the pools of these meta-morphic droplets.

He held them... and lost them... and sipped up what he could as they found their way home to earth.

In each liquid kiss he sensed rain's invisible intention to continue as far as possible to the center of this tiny planetsphere on the edge of a remote galaxy... until rising again in the veins of great living things, until becoming the re-greening of deserts and taking flight on the warm winds of these lands to re-become the sky.
This journey seemed to be whispering that transformation is the true path of consciousness... and that our lives, our energies, our loves and losses, our creations and destructions, our visions... we and they... all return home in a great confluence of spirit.

He looked around him. It was still morning. The desert land was gleaming with rare moisture and the cool air of possibility. He felt re-opened to his life and to how one day every particle of his being would return home, back to the embrace and the origin of rain.

QUESTIONS CONCERNING THE WEIGHT OF THINGS...

Today at sunset I counted 751 candles in a sea of wax on the Brooklyn Promenade. Each candle was carefully placed onto this alter of faith and sorrow, creating a vigil of fire to represent the flames of love, and the excruciating pain still burning in this city of millions. The wax flowed onto the concrete in an endless stream of molten tears for those who were so recently returned to the vapor of their souls.

Many of us gathered and stood there, belated witnesses and connected strangers, each replaying the visions and horrors of September 11th in an effort to remember and forget more than we ever could. We were all so quiet that I could hear the wind gently playing with a thousand love-and-loss paper-poems, tied, taped, and placed onto the wrought iron railings overlooking lower Manhattan. We were drenched in the quiet murmurs of sorrow and awe, in the ominous mechanical whir of cars on a highway literally below our feet... and I came away lighter and heavier, and in possession of these questions concerning the unknowable weight of things...

Like... like... What's the weight of faith in a river of tears that flow to an ocean of mourning? What's the weight of one lost soul within the broken heart of a mother's grief, of a father's silent tears for his son, or of a husband's endless lament for the loss of the love of his life? What's the weight of hope from the hopes of 3,000 people staring into the vacant eyes of hopelessness? What's the weight of sunset's blood-red, last rays of light, caressing the quiet faces and heavy hearts of so many mourners? What's the weight of a thousand-thousand flames dancing on the prayer candles of the missing and the dead?

What's the weight of the dust that fell back upon the people of New York City, and what is the power and weight of being kissed and covered by the dust that contained the essence of so many lives that were taken?

What is the weight of sorrow and the weight of fury? What is the weight of dreams that were lost, of journeys left incomplete, of children not born, of spirits restlessly searching the rubble of hate for what there would have been of love and wonder on this planet of misery and miracle?

What is the weight of our regrets, and the unfinished business of the souls of the dead?

What is the weight of a single moment of peace, or of a lifetime of war? What is the weight of 1000 bombs, and the weight of their destruction, and what is the weight of retribution? What is the weight of annihilation of a country and its people…or the loss of your child? What is the weight of our vision for the future? What is the weight of blind hate, or of a lover's last words to his beloved?

What is the weight of every crown ever worn, of every love ever lost, of every cross ever carried, of all the blood ever shed, or of every soldier's prayer to return home alive? What is the weight of the lasting vision of the last time we see someone before they die? What is the weight of a child's endless wonder and the endlessness of "never" when mommy's never coming home? What is the weight of unity and sorrow, of pride and sacrifice, of heroism and horror? What is the weight of one last dance, and of the first tentative sounds of laughter among our tears of mourning and anger among the blessings we give to one another? What is the weight of our human condition and the magnificence of our souls?

What is the weight of all this… and how much would it weigh when placed at the feet of God?

MY DREAMS TAKE ME OVER

My dreams… my dreams take me. My dreams take me over and deep into the world of before. Before this, before now, before knowing and into the endless inward spiral of forever. Over and over into the endless inward spiral. My dreams take me over and over, inward and inward to the deep and blinding darkness of forever and ever… unknowing.

These waters flow over me, endlessly over and overflow to the sweet liquid darkness of forever flowing, over and over, deep and deeper until my dreams take. me. Over.

Over the edge, over and above the clouds and over to the low side of a forgotten road. Over to the over-and-over of the moon's call to ocean waves as they lay their moving bodies down on the sweet shores of everywhere.

Over and over like the child in us all shouting for "again" and "again" and "again." Over and over like seeing those we love returning home.

Over.   and Over. Like my dreams
take me over.

WONDER AND MIRACLE

I am hurtling eastward, 543 miles per hour at 37,000 feet above the oceans of earth, simultaneously into the darkness and towards the light. Even in the 21st century this is an obscene speed and an unfathomable environment. While I am flying home filled with the wonders of our interconnected humanity, this flight is challenging my life-long perception of earth's exquisite balance of night and day.

We are traveling with the roll of our sweet blue planet, so the sun's journey across the sky is now in super-slo-mo. Our eight-hour flight has us arriving three clock hours after we departed. It's an an impossible equation…but it's true: eight hours in-the-sky as we cross four time zones and then dis-integrate into the lost hour of America's daylight savings.

The peoples on this flight descend from those now among the many nations once known as the great Mali Empire. As we leave from Africa, I can see and feel it, that this mix of humanity is a 21st century snapshot; a living webwork of our endless, shared connections. And while our human family has its beginnings in the African Motherlands, this mix of miracle beings, flying seven miles above the waters from which we once came, is telling us as much about where we've been as where we're going… Like, ready or not we're on this trip together and just like our minds and spirits, our fates are so truly inseparable.

When we arrive into NYC… most of these passengers, who are among the majority peoples of color on earth, will suddenly be swimming in the strange and often hostile waters of the American-born delusion/inversion of reality that they are a minority population. This mis-mind of our treasured togetherness hurts, and continues to do harm.

But for those who see… we are wondrous beings. The colors of our skins and clothing, the tangled webwork of our languages, the invisible and overlapping creation myths that speak in tongues of where we might or might not go from here… it's all about the marvel of us.

To me, we seem like a chaotic free-flowing, interconnected and highly differentiated organism with a great propensity towards awe and wonder when given the chance. The New Jersey born daredevil in me whispers "take your chances man… take your chances." But it's too late for whispers. This is a plane full of folks who have all taken the chance; we've all already taken the dare to go and let go.

As we "exit the vehicle" I admit that I try to do that with everything I touch. I take my chances with those I love, and they know it too. I'm all in… all in on them, on us, and wherever love takes us.

Humanity is my medicine. We are my ticket to an eternal running-flying-leaping-dive into an unshakeable faith that we will make magic with our minds and with the skills we have disappeared into. And the music… I guess the music will dance like it does far beyond what we've imagined.

So this wonderment of traveling at the edge of space in a tiny sliver of winged metal, filled with a cargo of rare beings from a tiny planet on the far edges of an obscure galaxy… it all seems to fit right in with my "take your chances" vision of reality.

Everything will surely happen.

Open **our** eyes. Open **our** minds… We are flying together above the surface of the third planet from our sun in one of the rarest of all atmospheres, created by the strangest confluence of fate and circumstance.

What more do you need to know of miracle… other than it's always time to take y**our** chances.

NIGHT SPIRITS

My hands are raised to the endless sky and I am dancing under an ocean of stars. Their gentle light is my guide through this moment. Night spirits whisper and sing a lullaby to entice my dreams to boldly come true and to help heal the sorrow and loss that have brought their feathery breath to my attention.

I am so very blessed with life in all its marvel. I am seeing the wondrous touch of love in everything. The infinite sky sends me on a rocket ride to the soft edges of eternity. The blinding sun shouts a bold invitation to the web-work of my connection with all things and to those I dare to truly love.

I hear an amen roll softly over my lips. It's more of an exclamation than the end of this prayer. I imagine I'm writing these words on a scrap of ancient parchment that I attach to the string of a kite that comes to rest in the hands of God.

We try so hard and so very sincerely to be the worthy sons and daughters of wonderment… and I confess…

I love us for that.

UNDERTOW OF SURVIVAL

Not so long ago he saw himself and his reflection in the blinding mirror of shame. He saw a servant of fear, a chameleon whose skin changed to the color and texture of every truth that threatened him. He became so many truths that there were none left for him to be made of. He took on the personas, the essence of these truths upon which he laid in a camouflage so profoundly complete that there was no finding himself. His ability to be anything threatened everything that he might be. The sweet pinpoint of exactly who he was now was being devoured by the near infinity of the possible. He had become what he imagined himself wanting to be, instead of riding the chemistry of desire and circumstance. And he continued like this until he fell into the endless hall of mirrors, until the disparate universe of his selves coalesced in the furious confluence of clouds that are the storm, the hurricane, the black funnel of destruction that we separate and save ourselves from… by naming it hell.

All this so that he would be born yet again, shrieking the first song that blesses our arrivals. He began to recognize his infinity to be this living body, and that he was the infinite genii of a moment, wrapped up in the fragile lamp of human form. All his secrets, all the treasures of the universe he embodied could be had by the careful rub of intimacy. He died the small death-dance of his efforts to be known; he suffered laying bare his palace of light and pain; he felt alone when only he was there for the sweet ride of his joy and sorrow, of his spirit become flesh. He was alone among so many, unable to recognize themselves in the shattered, exquisite hologram of humanity. The thousand-million faces of our souls shone in each drop of his blood, and the salt crystals of his sweat from the work of love were the diamonds of his world.

He drew a long, deep breath. He kissed his mind good night with a child's sense of wonder and fear that sleep was so much like death. He felt himself hoping this was not his last chance to relinquish the burden and blessing of being alive. He cried the blood, and he sweat the tears of his divinity until all that was left was the only man he ever was.

He was in New York City, home of the beatnik and spawning ground of be-bop and the many practitioners of hip. Hip language, hip culture, hip-hop, hip everything and anything. It was the home of the home of those brave enough to survive until sunrise. The red-orange sun was setting and its warmth was a kiss on the late-afternoon side of his face. The city wore this twilight glow with elegance…

Everything was alive in its blood-red aura. Westbound motorists were blinded to a courteous crawl… It was a Zen-trance sunset that infused them with something as close to love and respect for life as they could ever get on these stretches of hostile highway. Strange as it sounds, crowded cemeteries occasionally dotted this landscape; each of their many headstones was a prayer to the heavens as much as a prayer for each of us still here. And he was in need of prayer, and touch, and breathtaking love.

The entire city looked alive, like everything was breathing that soft rise and fall of a lover's breath in sleep. He laid his head on her heartbeat on this highway of dreams. The feel of her kiss was heavy in the air. The refuge she offered and needed was in her every breath…The embrace and luscious kiss of her mind was in the body fluid of this city, whose heartbeat was an irresistible invitation to entrainment.

Maybe he was home… maybe his journey was just beginning. Maybe it was the shape of their souls that set them in each other's orbit like two dancers creating one body of motion, a sacred confluence of two growing entities. Her touch, her taste, her smell, her movement, her voice; it was all an invitation.

He accepted.

He looked down from his rocket ride seat on US Air flight 300 to San Francisco. He saw the scattered clusters of light like neurological starbursts of human civilization. These patterns are the hieroglyphics of our need and desire to be in close contact with each other. Each light might as well be one soul… like a soft glow emanating from a planet whose love of it's own divine nature, it's own ebb and flow of survival, is expressed in silent witness of our arrivals and departures, our lives and our loves… our arrogance and our wonder at ourselves and all that surrounds us.

These lights and their patterns are the charged electrical essence of our spirits and our time in this place. Enough of us breathing, working, touching, loving; enough density of our existence in one place creates a critical mass of light, whose glow can be felt by the hands of lovers on each other's skin, and whose luminescence can only be seen at some great distance.

And the patterns of these patterns, flowing and overflowing as they do across the surface of this electric earth, would somehow spell our humanity if we could ever comprehend such a thing. And the long, dark, quiet stretches below, these tranquil seas of blackness that give birth to what we call light… these are the moments of such stillness, such peace, that we rarely recognize them even when they are upon us. They come after a heavy rain, before long journeys home, before we leave this life, and sometimes, just sometimes we find someone in whose arms such a moment is possible.

In those moments, we love ourselves so well, so fully that we can begin to see the wondrous glow of our own divinity; when our lives and the entirety of our human lineage appears as an infinite corridor of souls, a hall of mirrors that reflects and magnifies the blinding emanations of all life that has ever been.

And this magnificence, this is the work of a life force so vast we tend only to see its chaos and ominous grandeur. We live in it. We live from it. It is the entropic sea of energy from which we may take… nothing. Absolutely nothing.

Because we are the exquisite nothing, we are the void that allows for all things… we are the black night that becomes each day. We are part of all these things to which we sometimes give the name God. And if there is a God, it could be no other way than we would be imbued with such beauty. And if there is no God, well… then it could be no other way because we would need to be immersed in such beauty and magnificence just to survive.

LEGACY OF FREEDOM

We the people of America
like to call this the "Land of The Free."
And when it's real freedom,
freedom sets us all free
to stand by one another, to dare and then discover
how freedom sets us free to be
who and how we have come here to be.

Gotta gotta be free to let your freak-flag fly,
free to send your prayers up to the sky.
Freedom's a true and precious thing,
and I love the sounds of freedom's ring.
I dig the freedoms freedom brings.
I dig the words when we all sing
of how these freedoms ring so true
when they belong to me and you,
when we go beyond the things we know
just to let our love of freedom show.

Cause in the joy of freedom's dance every dancer has to have their chance to dance among We The People…or it ain't no dance at all.

No one dances in the sacred halls if the temple built on freedom falls,
if no one's there to call and answer the calls… for freedom.

Cause in the joy of freedom's reign can't be no shackles, can't be no chains on votes, on hopes, on who we love, on equal pay, on rising above from everywhere and everything, cause this is how our freedoms ring, and this is what our freedoms bring to you and me and We The People…

Look close, cause the face of America is me and you and everyone from the whole world-wide-world who dares to dare to build dreams true and remember all we've all been through…

Cause when we do…we make America…
more like the America we dream… as in "I have a dream today."

Yeah, I got a dream…

In my dream this sacred Earth is becoming
the lands of a world-wide free,
and all our tribes on this sweet planet
are part of our human family, a tapestry
in the ever-changing legacy… of

Free—ee-dom. Free—ee-dom.
Free—ee-dom. Free-dom, Free-dom.

Time to re-love, re-dance, re-imagine, re-sing,
time to re-build just about everything.
Time to dare to re-set justice free,
just to see what we can be… together.

Gotta keep the love, keep the courage, keep the faith.
Keep the brother-and-sisterhood of every race.
Keep the vision to be the land of the free
and dare to re-envision our democracy.

Set your mind on fire. Set your mind on free.
Set your mind on freeing our democracy.
Set your mind on fire. Set your mind on free.
Set your mind on freeing our democracy.

Look out baby…Democracy is re-coming to America.
"It'll soon shake your windows and rattle your walls, for the…"

Time to light the fires of freedom's ring,
rock the rhythms and rhymes, raise our voices and sing
of how freedom's fire dares everything
to glow with all that real freedom brings.

Set your mind on fire. Set your mind on free.

I JUST GO MISSING...

Some days I just go missing... missing in the sweet flow of my mostly charmed life, or missing amid the chaotic wonder of an entire universe overflowing in the spectacle of our nomadic humanity. While I feel fully present and accounted for, in those moments it just seems like I've meandered off the main drag and onto an uncharted footpath, allured by the faint glow of my own soul just beyond the near horizon.

In this way I am so very truly one of us; hard wired to override any and all reason and reasonable doubt in the instinct-driven pursuit of unpossessable shinning things.

I'm in love with the mesmerizing twinkle of distant stars, with sunlight on frozen landscapes, with how the sky looks when I open my eyes underwater, with what our backlit dancing shadows can do on the surface of a pond, and with the sparkle of tears of joy in my lover's eyes.

I see evidence of an unknowable eternity in everything we touch and in everything that touches us, and I am attempting to live under-the-influence of all this... and then somehow surf on the ferocious waves of love and loss that caress what I know of life. It's like I'm a lone drop of water in free fall over the edge where all waters fall, disintegrating in a thunder of oneness.

And just like that... I rejoin the waters of my beginnings, I let go of my moment of singularity and just go... missing. Missing among the mystic waters, missing in the chaotic wonder of ageless aging... I just go missing in the forever lost and found of consciousness... of gratitude... and of love for our exquisite, unfinished humanity.

THE GREAT REJOINING

I stand before the universe, before the entirety of creation. It's as if every cell of me wants to let go of its current form and rejoin the free-flow cosmos. I can actually see myself returning to the liquid stardust from which I came, and it seems so very real, and so very far beyond anything I've experienced.

I feel it like I have felt my lover's whisper on the skin of my ear.

As each particle of me celebrates its return home, I'm wondering where the love that possesses me will go in this great unwinding… where the double-helix DNA that is my living signature will be when ebb and flow become one.

What becomes of our minds and spirits? What of the invisible magnificence of living entities? Where is the space for that which has no location and seems not to need or recognize space itself?

As far as I can tell we are the charmed raveling of a universe of possibilities, woven into sentient being by fate and outrageous circumstance, and then stranger even than that… we've fallen in love with our mindfulness, and now we are reaching out to know the unknowably endless workings of our unfathomable beginnings.

We are tugging on the pant legs of the Great and All Powerful OZ, protected only by the paper-thin membrane of our curiosity for the answer to a million great questions… that somehow come down to our one-and-only question…

"How do you work all this stuff? Somebody?… anybody. I could use some help here… How do you work this thing?"

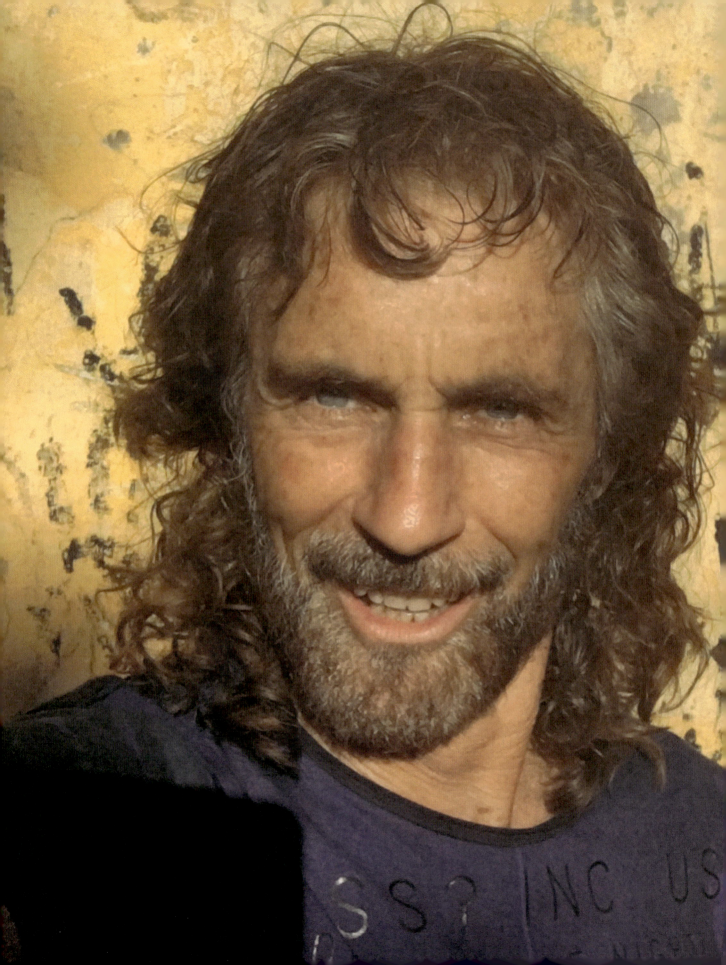

AIR PILGRIMAGE

I'm going 467 mph in this steel-bird, this air-bus to the edge of marvel... I'm in the narrow, ethereal, and well defined strip between the low and high clouds of earth... I feel suspended between waking and dreaming realities. I am literally somewhere between earth and all that is beyond what little I can say I know.

Above me are the last silky fingers of our precious atmosphere as they fade into space. Below me are the sunrise-lit thunderclouds of our breathing planet. The roar of the engines, the sound and smell of activity around me have somehow become the dispensable candy of my senses. But they are nowhere near as sweet as loving and being loved by all who surround me on this third planet from the center of our illuminated universe.

And at the center of this center, my heart beats, my blood runs, and I spin stories of sound and words from all I see and sense. From the center of this center, I dare to run my hands through the treasures of love for those I allow to stand so close to me that they feel my breath on their skin.

The universe of my senses sweeps me up and away and next thing I know, I'm looking down onto this miracle earth through the dreamy powder blue of the infinite heavens. I'm staring into the imperceivable confluence where the ocean meets the sky...where the waters of this water world drift upwards and literally disappear into thin air to become the clouds. It's a journey, a pilgrimage that I imagine my soul will someday make as I leave my body of knowledge to join the entropic, collective soul of all who were once here among the wondrous and unforgiving elements.

And the creatures who inhabit this place... the truth tellers and potion-sellers, the hucksters, bamboozlers and sooth-sayers; the poets, the visionaries and the warriors... we seem to be accidentally dancing with each other in celebration of our ferocious lunge at survival.

Our ragtag, random tribe of humanity sits quietly within this flying machine that is eating a path through the sky... The balance of our collective human purposes here on US Air flight 307 seems so small, so superfluous, but these purposes, nefarious and wonderful, are the fuel for this nearly unimaginable journey across our sky. They have reawakened my wonderment and my awareness of the legacy of our truly exquisite human condition.

In the smallness of our individual realities, there is a kind of peace and quiet; an unknowable comfort with our place in a vast universe. We are so supremely insignificant. But if everything matters… if every change really changes everything… then just maybe by playing our infinitesimal parts in the great tangled webwork of all things… maybe… maybe we matter a great deal.

And of all things ever to come to being, of all the stranger than strange impossibilities, seems like we are the least possible, the most unlikely and rarest of rare beings. Seems like we are living proof of a functional zero coming to pass.

So… yeah you can say it… We. Are. A. Cosmic. Miracle.

Which is why, way up here on flight 307… it's why our hope matters, why our choices matter, why our pain and our exquisite love matters, and why our collective visions and wisdom are the true refuge of our precious human being.

PLANET OF MIRACLES

Looking for mercy in the strong arms of sleep,
beaten down by another day and just hoping to keep
on track, on time, in love, in line…
eyes to the stars, I'm desperately trying
to keep my mind on sanity…

I scan the horizon for signs of my life,
for a familiar face or a warm fire's light,
for some vision or voice to guide my way,
an embrace in this darkness that will sirvive the day
and the madness of being abandoned in love,
and of falling so far there's no rising above
the pain and the sorrow of love badly lost.
So I dare to curse God for my feeling star-crossed.

In a moment so full, so empty, so low,
I stop sweating my death, my loss, and I know
I'm going to die. I'm going to lose all I've got,
that's why I live like I live, that's why I'm not
holding back, I'm not waiting to speak
my mind or my heart, I'm here to seek
and be found, to know and be known,
to love, to loose, to show and be shown
the wonders of this place so wonders-full,
and the amazing graces of our miracles.

Show me your miracles and I'll show you mine.
On this planet of miracles all we have is the time
to do what it is we've come here to do,
to live and love well, to survive and stay true
to the sweet bold oneness of daring to be who
we are…

Sometimes I'm the child, lost and alone.
Sometimes I'm the wild sea, crushing the bones
of sailors who dare to challenge me.
Sometimes I'm the father dying before I see
my son grown…

Sometimes I'm a witness to the heroic pain
of genuine forgiveness under the torrential rain
of love…. generous and true.
Sometimes that's me… sometimes it's you.
Sometimes I'm the nomad, the earth is my home,
sometimes I'm the bag-lady, lost and alone,
sometimes I'm a tear on the shoe of a man
who's lost all he's had, who's done all he can.

Sometimes… sometimes…
Sometimes a rain of sorrow soaks me to the bone.
I stare at the night until tomorrow, alone
with what burns my heart and spirit.
I search for home, but I'm nowhere near its
soothing vibe, and familiar embrace,
I'm lost and hoping to find some trace
of me.

I've had days when even Hell's demons have mercy
and days when the angels want to be me,
I've had nights, sweet and dark when troubles were still,
I've known nights that were years of pain that I will
remember.

Show me your miracles and I'll show you mine.
On this planet of miracles, all we have is the time
to do what it is we've come here to do,
to live and love well, to survive and stay true
to the sweet bold oneness of daring to be who
we are…
Show me your miracles and I'll show you mine.
On this planet of miracles, all we have is time.
Show me your miracles and I'll show you mine.
On this planet of miracles, all we have is time.

IT'S GOING TO HAPPEN

I say it's time to jump into the deep end of the pool… into the deep end of our humanity. It's time to jump into the deep waters and rescue our luminous souls.

I'm not buying that we're all about to be consumed in the flames of hell here. It's the other way around. The mantra of the cosmos is and has always been that "All Things Are Possible."

The blinding light of life and consciousness sends us, ready or not, careening into an unknowable future… where the totality of our visions and actions becomes the fiery matrix of our ever-changing evolution…

I'm pretty sure by now you can hear it… I'm just shouting to myself and to all of us that this is the time to fully commit to who we know we can be. This is the time to commit to our visions for ourselves and fully engage the engine of our energies to fling us into the next phase of humanity. And it's going to happen with or without these words of my impassioned call.

It's going to happen.

Tony Vacca has been a free lance percussionist/poet for over four decades. He's performed and/or recorded with: Pop icon Sting, Jazz and World Music legends Don Cherry, Yusef Lateef and Avery Sharpe, with world renowned Senegalese vocalist Baaba Maal, with American born vocalist/percussionist Vinx, and with American poets Abiodun Oyewole (of The Last Poets), Ms. Tantra Zawadi, and America's Beat Poet laureate, Paul Richmond.

All this in addition to his work as a soloist and his performing projects that include World Rhythms Ensemble, The Senegal-America Project, Fusion Nomads, Impulse Ensemble, and Do It Now. While all seven of his World Fusion recordings to date include spoken word tracks, two of these feature his original word creations. They are "Zen Rant" and "The Rescue of Luminous Being." These and all his recordings to date are available on his Bandcamp site at: tonyvacca.bandcamp.com.

For more: www.tonyvacca.com